BOSTON
Red Sox

BY K. C. KELLEY

The Child's World®

Published by The Child's World®
1980 Lookout Drive • Mankato, MN 56003-1705
800-599-READ • www.childsworld.com

Acknowledgments
The Child's World®: Mary Berendes, Publishing Director
Red Line Editorial: Editorial direction
The Design Lab: Design
Amnet: Production
Design Elements: Photodisc

Photographs ©: Matt Trommer/Shutterstock Images, cover, 1, 2;
Michael Tureski/Icon SMI, 5; Steven King/Icon SMI, 6, 25 (top);
McGreevey Collection/Wikimedia Commons, 9; Michael Dwyer/
AP Images, 10; Eric Broder Van Dyke/Shutterstock Images, 13;
Design Lab, 14; Daniel Gluskoter/Icon SMI, 17; Rusty Kennedy/
AP Images, 18; Manuel Balce Ceneta/AP Images, 21; Preston
Stroup/AP Images, 22; AP Images, 22 (inset); Mark Goldman/
Icon SMI, 25 (center); Zuma Press/Icon SMI, 25 (bottom); Duane
Burleson/AP Images, 26; Seth Wenig/AP Images, 27

ISBN 9781623239749
LCCN 2013947261

Printed in the United States of America
Mankato, MN
December, 2013
PA02188

ABOUT THE AUTHOR

K. C. Kelley has written dozens of books on baseball and other sports for young readers. He has also been a youth baseball coach and called baseball games on the radio. His favorite team is the Boston Red Sox.

Cover: Clay Buchholz, Pitcher

C O N T E N T S

Go, Red Sox!

The Boston Red Sox are one of baseball's most famous teams. For more than 80 years they were famous for not winning the **World Series**. Their fans kept cheering for them, though. In recent years, the Red Sox have been one of baseball's best teams. They even won the World Series in 2013. Let's meet the Red Sox!

The Boston Red Sox celebrate winning the 2013 World Series.

Who Are the Red Sox?

The Boston Red Sox are a team in baseball's American League (AL). The AL joins with the National League (NL) to form Major League Baseball. The Red Sox play in the East Division of the AL. The division winners and two wild-card teams get to play in the league playoffs. The playoff winners from the two leagues face off in the World Series. The Red Sox have won eight World Series championships.

Shane Victorino and Dustin Pedroia are top Red Sox players.

Where They Came From

The Boston Red Sox haven't always been the Red Sox. They have, however, always played in Boston. The team started in 1901. They were called the Americans until 1908. From 1918 through 2003, they didn't win any World Series. In 2004, they finally won one!

The Boston Americans played against the Pittsburgh Pirates in the 1903 World Series.

Who They Play

The Boston Red Sox play 162 games each season. That includes about 19 games against each of the other teams in their division. The Red Sox have won seven AL East championships. The other AL East teams are the Baltimore Orioles, the New York Yankees, the Tampa Bay Rays, and the Toronto Blue Jays. The Red Sox and the Yankees are baseball's biggest rivals. Their games always get the fans charged up! These two teams have even battled in the playoffs. The Red Sox also play some teams from the NL. Their NL **opponents** change every year.

Dustin Pedroia receives a throw to try to tag a Yankees player out at second base.

Where They Play

Fenway Park is baseball's oldest ballpark. It opened in 1912. Fans everywhere love Fenway for its old-time style. The outside is made of bricks. The left-field wall is 37 feet (11 m) tall, the biggest in baseball. The wall is called The Green Monster! Since 2003, fans have been able to sit above the Monster. Before every game, the streets around Fenway Park fill with fans. They eat hot dogs, buy souvenirs, and share their love of the Sox!

Fenway Park has been home to the Red Sox since 1912.

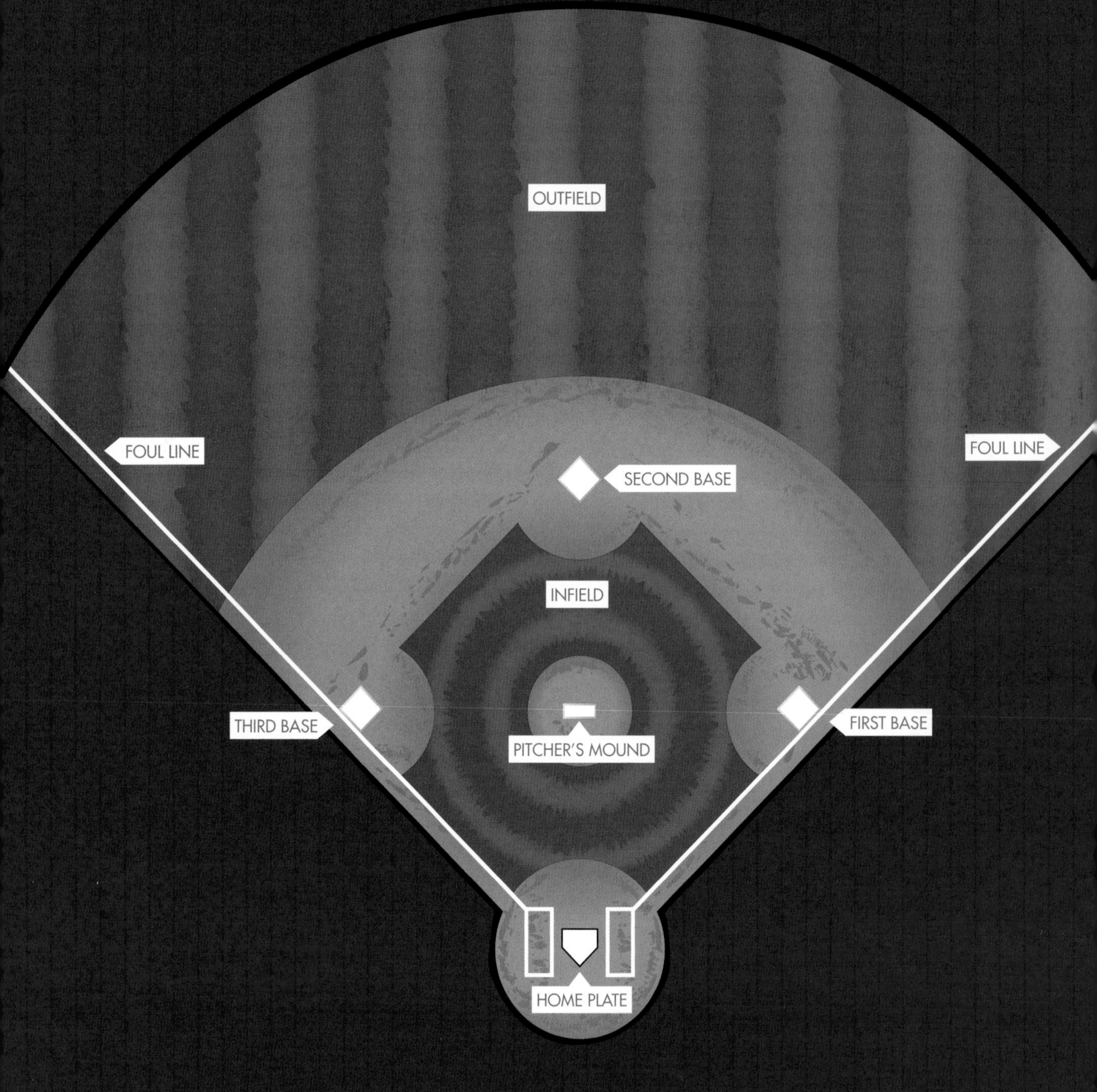

OUTFIELD

FOUL LINE

FOUL LINE

SECOND BASE

INFIELD

THIRD BASE

FIRST BASE

PITCHER'S MOUND

HOME PLATE

The Baseball Diamond

Baseball games are played on a field called a diamond. Four bases form this diamond shape. The bases are 90 feet (27 m) apart. The area around and inside the bases is called the infield. At the center of the infield is the pitcher's mound. The grass area beyond the bases is called the outfield. White lines start at **home plate** and go toward the outfield. These are the foul lines. Baseballs hit outside these lines are out of play unless a fielder catches them. The outfield walls are about 300–450 feet (91–137 m) from home plate.

Big Days

The Red Sox have had some great seasons in their history. Here are four of them:

1918: *The Red Sox won their third World Series in four years. They were led by Babe Ruth. The future home-run star was a great pitcher for Boston.*

2004: *After 86 years, the Red Sox finally won another World Series title. To reach the Series, they had to win four straight games against the rival Yankees. Then they beat the St. Louis Cardinals to win the Series.*

2007: *They did it again! With top pitchers and great hitting, the Red Sox won another World Series. This time, they beat the Colorado Rockies.*

2013: *The Red Sox finished last in the AL East in 2012. They rebounded in 2013 to win another World Series championship. They beat the St. Louis Cardinals to win.*

After 86 years without a championship, the Red Sox finally won the 2004 World Series.

Tough Days

The Red Sox have had a lot of tough seasons. Here are three of the worst:

1919: *The Red Sox sell the rights to Babe Ruth to the Yankees. Ruth goes on to become one of baseball's all-time greats, and the Red Sox fail to win a World Series for more than 80 years.*

1946: *The St. Louis Cardinals beat the Red Sox in Game 7 of the World Series. It was Boston's only chance in the World Series from 1918 until 1967.*

1986: *The Red Sox were one out away from winning the World Series. Then the New York Mets came from behind to win Game 6. The Mets also won Game 7 to take the series.*

Red Sox first baseman Bill Buckner reacts after making an error in Game 6 of the 1986 World Series.

Meet the Fans

The Red Sox play in Boston, but their fans live everywhere. So many people love the team that they are called the "Red Sox Nation." The six states in New England are packed with Sox fans. People who moved away from the area still follow the team, too.

The Red Sox even set a record by selling out 820 home games in a row! Fans fill Yawkey Way outside Fenway Park. The street was named for a former Red Sox owner.

Fans young and old love to watch the Red Sox!

Carl Yastrzemski, Outfield

Heroes Then . . .

Cy Young won 511 games, more than any other pitcher. He has a pitching award named after him. He threw the first perfect game of the 20th century. Tris Speaker was one of the best defensive outfielders ever. Babe Ruth was a famous slugger with the Yankees, but he began as a star pitcher for Boston in 1914. Ted Williams is called "the best hitter who ever lived." He hit .406 in 1941. No player has topped him since then. Carl "Yaz" Yastrzemski took over for Williams in left field. He won the Triple Crown in 1967 by leading the AL in batting average, home runs, and runs batted in. Jim Rice stepped in for Yaz in the 1980s and also had a Hall of Fame career. Pitcher Roger Clemens won three **Cy Young Awards** before leaving the Red Sox in 1997.

The great Ted Williams was one of the best hitters of all time.

Heroes Now . . .

Jon Lester is one of baseball's best pitchers. He joined Boston in 2006 and helped them win the 2007 World Series. He is joined by young pitching star Clay Buchholz. Second baseman Dustin Pedroia was the 2008 **Most Valuable Player**. Outfielder Jacoby Ellsbury is a top base stealer. Slugger David "Big Papi" Ortiz is a powerful hitter who won the **Hank Aaron Award** in 2005. He also led the AL in home runs and runs batted in during the 2006 season. Former team pitching coach John Farrell is now the **manager**.

The present-day Red Sox are loaded with star players.

Jon Lester, Pitcher

Jacoby Ellsbury, Outfield

Dustin Pedroia, Second Base

BAT

BATTING GLOVES

BATTING HELMET

TEAM JERSEY

TEAM PANTS

26

BASEBALL CLEATS

Gearing Up

Baseball players all wear a team jersey and pants. They have to wear a team hat in the field and a helmet when batting. Take a look at David Ortiz and Ryan Lavarnway to see some other parts of a baseball player's uniform.

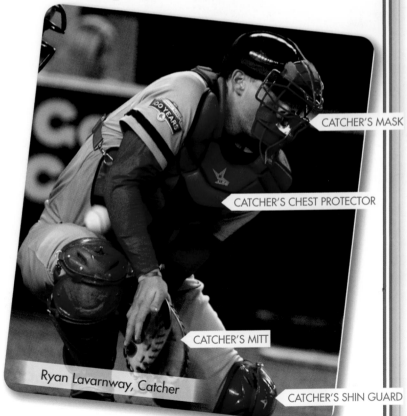

CATCHER'S MASK

CATCHER'S CHEST PROTECTOR

CATCHER'S MITT

CATCHER'S SHIN GUARD

Ryan Lavarnway, Catcher

On the left: David Ortiz, Designated Hitter

Sports Stats

Here are some all-time career records for the Boston Red Sox. All the stats are through the 2013 season.

THE BASEBALL

A Major League baseball weighs about 5 ounces (142 g). It is 9 inches (23 cm) around. A leather cover surrounds hundreds of feet of string. That string is wound around a small center of rubber and cork.

HOME RUNS

Ted Williams, 521
Carl Yastrzemski, 452

RUNS BATTED IN

Carl Yastrzemski, 1,844
Ted Williams, 1,839

BATTING AVERAGE

Ted Williams, .344
Wade Boggs, .338

STOLEN BASES

Harry Hooper, 300
Tris Speaker, 267

WINS BY A PITCHER

Cy Young, 192
Roger Clemens, 192

WINS BY A MANAGER

Joe Cronin, 1,071

EARNED RUN AVERAGE

Smoky Joe Wood, 1.99
Cy Young, 2.00

Glossary

Cy Young Awards awards given to the top pitcher in each league. Pitcher Roger Clemens won three Cy Young Awards with the Sox.

Hank Aaron Award an award given to the top overall hitter in each league. Slugger David Ortiz won the Hank Aaron Award in 2005.

home plate a five-sided rubber pad where batters stand to swing. Runners touch home plate to score runs.

manager the person in charge of the team and who chooses who will bat and pitch. Former pitching coach John Farrell is now the Sox manager.

Most Valuable Player a yearly award given to the top player in each league. Second baseman Dustin Pedroia was the 2008 Most Valuable Player.

opponents the teams or players that play against each other. The Sox's NL opponents change every year.

World Series the Major League Baseball championship. The World Series is played each year between the winners of the American and National Leagues.

Find Out More

BOOKS

Buckley, James Jr. *Eyewitness Baseball*.
New York: DK Publishing, 2010.

Stewart, Mark. *Boston Red Sox*. Chicago:
Norwood House Press, 2008.

Teitelbaum, Michael. *Baseball*. Ann Arbor,
MI: Cherry Lake Publishing, 2009.

WEB SITES

Visit our Web page for links about the Boston Red Sox and
other pro baseball teams: *www.childsworld.com/links*

*Note to Parents, Teachers, and Librarians: We routinely verify our
Web links to make sure they are safe, active sites—so encourage your
readers to check them out!*

Index